STARK COUNTY DIS

W9-BYS-546

APR   2012

Table of Contents

visit us at www.abdopublishing.com

Published by ABDO Publishing Company, a division of ABDO, P.O. Box 398166, Minneapolis, Minnesota 55439. Copyright © 2012 by Abdo Consulting Group, Inc. International copyrights reserved in all countries. No part of this book may be reproduced in any form without written permission from the publisher. SandCastle™ is a trademark and logo of ABDO Publishing Company.

Printed in the United States of America, North Mankato, Minnesota
102011
012012

  PRINTED ON RECYCLED PAPER

Editor: Liz Salzmann
Content Developer: Nancy Tuminelly
Cover and Interior Design and Production: Oona Gaarder-Juntti, Mighty Media, Inc.
Photo Credits: Digital Vision, Pixland, Shutterstock, Thinkstock

Library of Congress Cataloging-in-Publication Data
Hengel, Katherine.
  Senses are for everything : the five senses / Katherine Hengel.
    p. cm. -- (All about your senses)
  ISBN 978-1-61783-201-7
  1. Sense organs--Juvenile literature. 2. Senses and sensation--Juvenile literature. I. Title.
QP434.H46 2012
612.8--dc23
                        2011023503

SandCastle™ Level: Transitional

SandCastle™ books are created by a team of professional educators, reading specialists, and content developers around five essential components—phonemic awareness, phonics, vocabulary, text comprehension, and fluency—to assist young readers as they develop reading skills and strategies and increase their general knowledge. All books are written, reviewed, and leveled for guided reading, early reading intervention, and Accelerated Reader® programs for use in shared, guided, and independent reading and writing activities to support a balanced approach to literacy instruction. The SandCastle™ series has four levels that correspond to early literacy development. The levels are provided to help teachers and parents select appropriate books for young readers.

Emerging Readers
(no flags)

Beginning Readers
(1 flag)

Transitional Readers
(2 flags)

Fluent Readers
(3 flags)

SandCastle™

All About Your Senses

Senses
Are for Everything

THE FIVE SENSES

Katherine Hengel

Consulting Editor, Diane Craig, M.A./Reading Specialist

A Division of ABDO

ABDO
Publishing Company

Senses

Are for Everything

Senses help us understand our world. We use our senses all the time! Most people have five senses.

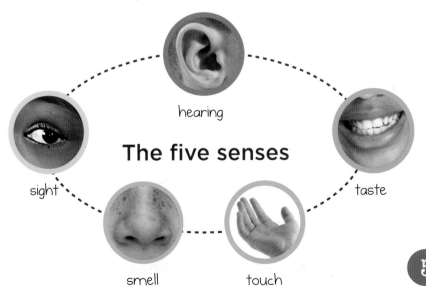

hearing

The five senses

sight

taste

smell

touch

Our Sense of Hearing

Derrick listens to Aaron's plan. Derrick can hear other noises in the classroom too.

Our ears sense sounds. Our brains tell us what the sounds mean. That's how we hear!

Our Sense of Sight

Miranda practices **juggling** a soccer ball. Her favorite player does it all the time! Miranda uses sight to watch the ball.

Our eyes send pictures to our brains. Our brains tell us what the pictures mean. That's how we see!

Our Sense of
Touch

Stephanie is at the beach. The sand feels **rough**. She's burying her dad's legs in the sand!

Our skin is covered with **sense receptors**. When things touch our skin, the receptors send messages to our brains. Our brains tell us what they mean. That's how we feel!

Our Sense of Taste

Cynthia's aunt got her an ice-cream cone. She takes a lick. It tastes like chocolate!

The roof of your mouth and your tongue are covered with **taste buds**. They send messages to your brain. Your brain tells you what they mean. That's how we taste!

Our Sense of Smell

Gabriel went to the **bakery** with his grandpa. He got two muffins! One is lemon and the other is chocolate. They smell so fresh!

Odors go into our noses. Our noses have **sense receptors**. The sense receptors send messages to our brains. Our brains tell us what they mean. That's how we smell!

Senses
Work Together

Bailey feels the wind in her hair. She can smell her neighbor's campfire too.

Our five senses work together. We can use more than one at once!

Senses

Work Together

Anthony is nervous. He needs one more strike! He can hear the crowd cheering. He can see the batter at home plate. He can smell the leather of his glove.

Senses

Work Together

Leah is in the ocean. She can taste the salt water. She can hear the waves! What else can she sense?

Facts About Senses

◆ Our sense **organs** send messages to our brains. It happens without us even knowing!

◆ We have five main sense organs. They are the eyes, nose, ears, tongue, and skin.

◆ Each sense uses its own special part of the brain.

Senses Quiz

1. Our ears send pictures to our brains. True or false?

2. Our skin is covered with **sense receptors**. True or false?

3. Only the roof of the mouth has **taste buds**. True or false?

4. We can use more than one sense at once. True or false?

Answers 1. False 2. True 3. False 4. True

23

Glossary

bakery – a place where breads and pastries are made.

juggle – to keep something in the air by hitting it with the hands, knees, or feet.

organ – a body part that does a specific job for the body.

rough – not smooth or soft.

sense receptor – one of the tiny parts of the body that senses things, such as odors, and sends the information to the brain.

taste bud – one of the tiny bumps in the mouth that sense what things taste like.